本冊 Lesson 1 の英文をもう一度読んで，次の活動に取り組みましょう。

Words and Phrases 英文中に出てきた語句・表現について，それぞれ左側の空所には英語を，右側の空所には日本語の意味を書き入れましょう。

1. _____ 形 [A2] 国際的な

2. be expected to ~ _____

3. major in ... _____

4. register 動 [B1] _____

5. previous 形 [B1] _____

6. _____ 名 [A2] 貿易

7. industry 名 [B1] _____

8. literature 名 [B1] _____

9. feel free to ~ _____

10. _____ 名 [B2]

Questions 次の問いに英語で答えましょう。

1. Who is this notice for?

_____

2. What are many of the international high school students at the event interested in?

_____

3. When will the international high school students have the lecture on "World Literature"?

_____

4. Who will give the lectures during the event?

_____

Express Yourself ティーチングアシスタントに応募するEメールを送ろうと思います。応募したい理由を，30～40語程度の英語で書いてみましょう。

Subject:	Application for a teaching assistant position
From:	
To:	Julia Taylor <juliataylor@daiichiuniversity.edu>

Dear Ms. Taylor,

I would like to work as a teaching assistant.

_____

_____

_____

Thank you for considering my application.   I would appreciate the opportunity to work as a teaching assistant in your program and look forward to hearing from you soon.

Sincerely,

HINTS 自分が大学生になったつもりで，高校生との活動を通して学びたいことや，「高校生に大学での勉強がどのようなものか伝えたい」など，高校生にしてあげたいことを考えてみましょう。

Helpful Expressions be of value to me「私にとって価値がある」
have back ground knowledge about ...「…についての背景知識がある」
have previous experience as ...「以前に…としての経験がある」

本冊 Lesson 2 の英文をもう一度読んで，次の活動に取り組みましょう。

Words and Phrases 英文中に出てきた語句・表現について，それぞれ左側の空所には英語を，右側の空所には日本語の意味を書き入れましょう。

1. be happy to ～　.....................

2. .... 動 [A1] …を集める

3. .... 名 [A2] 料金

4. trash 名 [B1]　.....................

5. throw away ...　.....................

6. be worn out　.....................

7. donate 動 [B2]　.....................

8. print ... out　.....................

9. make sure to ～　.....................

10. sign 動 [B1]　.....................

Questions 次の問いに英語で答えましょう。

1. When will the first event of the Endless Summer Festival be held?

....

2. What can people do at the second event?

....

3. When did the Endless Summer Festival start?

....

4. If you donate your old clothes at the Endless Summer Festival, what will Endless Summer do with them?

....

Express Yourself Endless Summer Festival に参加するために，次の申込書を記入する必要があります。必要事項を30語程度の英語で記入してみましょう。

Endless Summer Festival Application Form

1. Name: ....

2. Why do you want to join our festival?

....

....

....

3. Do you want to sell or donate clothes?

[☑Yes. / ☐No.　I would like to buy used clothes.]

Helpful Expressions support an environmentally-friendly event「環境にやさしいイベントを支持する」
contribute to ...「…に貢献する」　reduce waste「ごみを減らす」

本冊 Lesson 3 の英文をもう一度読んで，次の活動に取り組みましょう。

Words and Phrases

英文中に出てきた語句・表現について，それぞれ左側の空所には英語を，右側の空所には日本語の意味を書き入れましょう。

1. ＿＿＿＿＿＿ 名 [A2] 賞　　　　　　6. point of view ＿＿＿＿＿＿

2. be organized by ... ＿＿＿＿＿＿　　7. ＿＿＿＿＿＿ 名 [A2] もの

3. occasion 名 [B1] ＿＿＿＿＿＿　　　8. objective 形 [B2] ＿＿＿＿＿＿

4. fall in love ＿＿＿＿＿＿　　　　　9. conduct 動 [B2] ＿＿＿＿＿＿

5. ＿＿＿＿＿＿ 動 [A2] …を探究する　10. be related to ... ＿＿＿＿＿＿

Questions

次の問いに英語で答えましょう。

1. According to the poster, when did the Leonard Library Book Award officially start?

＿＿＿＿＿＿＿＿＿＿＿＿＿＿＿＿＿＿＿＿＿

2. What can we listen to during this year's event?

＿＿＿＿＿＿＿＿＿＿＿＿＿＿＿＿＿＿＿＿＿

3. Who is probably going to talk about how to read books?

＿＿＿＿＿＿＿＿＿＿＿＿＿＿＿＿＿＿＿＿＿

4. Where will the event take place?

＿＿＿＿＿＿＿＿＿＿＿＿＿＿＿＿＿＿＿＿＿

Express Yourself

あなたのお気に入りの本の紹介文 (a review of your favorite book) を，40～50語程度の英語で書いてみましょう。

Do you have a book to share?　Tell us about it!

My Favorite Book: ＿＿＿＿＿＿＿＿＿＿

＿＿＿＿＿＿＿＿＿＿＿＿＿＿＿＿＿＿＿＿＿

＿＿＿＿＿＿＿＿＿＿＿＿＿＿＿＿＿＿＿＿＿

＿＿＿＿＿＿＿＿＿＿＿＿＿＿＿＿＿＿＿＿＿

＿＿＿＿＿＿＿＿＿＿＿＿＿＿＿＿＿＿＿＿＿

HINTS　紹介文を読んだ人がその本を読みたくなるような文を書くことを目指しましょう。

Helpful Expressions　The book I would like to share with you is ... 「私があなたと共有したい本は…」
This is the story of ... 「これは…の話です」
This book tells us that ... 「この本は私たちに…を教えてくれます」

Words and Phrases 英文中に出てきた語句・表現について，それぞれ左側の空所には英語を，
右側の空所には日本語の意味を書き入れましょう。

1. have access to ...　_____
2. be concerned about ...　_____
3. considerable 形 [B1]　_____
4. _____　名 [A2] 予算
5. retain 動 [B1]　_____

6. become addicted to ...　_____
7. be tempted to ～　_____
8. _____　形 [A1] 個人的な
9. stick to ...　_____
10. _____　名 [A2] 教育

Questions 次の問いに英語で答えましょう。

1. What are some schools in Japan considering?

   _____

2. According to the passage, why do teachers need to attend training programs after
   introducing tablet computers in their school?

   _____

3. Why does Sophia think students should read printed textbooks?

   _____

4. What does Daniel call education styles that don't use tablet computers or digital
   textbooks?

   _____

Express Yourself 次の質問について，あなたの考えを40〜50語程度の英語で書いてみましょう。

Question: What are the benefits of introducing tablet computers into the classroom?

_____

_____

_____

_____

HINTS The biggest advantage [One of the advantages] of introducing tablet computers into the classroom is ... という書き出しで書
いてみよう。

Helpful Expressions on one's tablet computers「タブレットパソコンで」
paper handouts「紙のプリント」

Lesson 5

本冊Lesson 5の英文をもう一度読んで，次の活動に取り組みましょう。

Words and Phrases 英文中に出てきた語句・表現について，それぞれ左側の空所には英語を，右側の空所には日本語の意味を書き入れましょう。

1. be classified as ... _____
2. be in danger of ... _____
3. _____ 動 [A2] …を明らかにする
4. capture 動 [B1] _____
5. hit upon ... _____

6. entire 形 [B1] _____
7. track 動 [B2] _____
8. migration 名 [B2] _____
9. destruction 名 [B1] _____
10. habitat 名 [B1] _____

Questions 次の問いに英語で答えましょう。

1. How many species of sea turtles are there in the world?

_____

2. Why do some species of sea turtles swim thousands of miles during their lifetime?

_____

_____

3. How did Wallace J. Nichols track Adelita?

_____

4. According to the passage, what did millions of kids do by using the Internet?

_____

Express Yourself 次の質問について，あなたの考えを40〜50語程度の英語で書いてみましょう。

Question: Why are some marine animals in danger of extinction?　Think about the reasons and ways to protect them.

_____

_____

_____

_____

HINTS 海洋生物を脅かしている理由としては，海洋汚染や乱獲が考えやすいものとしてあげられます。解決するために何ができるかについても考えてみましょう。

Helpful Expressions a huge amount of waste「ばく大な量のごみ」
be in danger of extinction「絶滅の危機にある」
excessive hunting「乱獲」　　hunt excessively「乱獲する」
marine [sea water] pollution「海洋汚染」

本冊 Lesson 6 の英文をもう一度読んで，次の活動に取り組みましょう。

Words and Phrases　英文中に出てきた語句・表現について，それぞれ左側の空所には英語を，
右側の空所には日本語の意味を書き入れましょう。

1. _____ 名 [A1] 汚染

2. current 形 [B1] _____

3. consume 動 [B1] _____

4. _____ 名 [A2] 便利さ

5. deal with ... _____

6. issue 名 [A2] _____

7. ban 名 [B2] _____

8. come into effect _____

9. supply 動 [B2] _____

10. restriction 名 [B2] _____

Questions　次の問いに英語で答えましょう。

1. According to Takuro's article, what is a big problem around the world?

_____

2. What is the main purpose of the action mentioned in the article?

_____

3. According to Prof. Adger's reply, what do the environmentalists call for?

_____

4. What are Takuro and his classmates going to do in Prof. Adger's next class?

_____

Express Yourself　あなたは次のテーマについてディスカッションをします。あなたの考えを
40～50語程度の英語で書いてみましょう。

　About eight million tons of plastic products go into the ocean every year, and they remain there forever.　What can you do about plastic pollution in the ocean?

_____

_____

_____

HINTS　ディスカッションなどで自分の意見を述べるときは，In my opinion, ... などで文を始めるとよいでしょう。続いて，プラスチック製品の使用を避けることや，リサイクルをすることなど，自分に何ができるか意見を述べましょう。

Helpful Expressions　avoid using ... 「…を使うことを避ける」
plastic waste doesn't decompose in the ocean 「プラスチックごみは海で分解されない」
what we can do is ... 「私たちができることは…」

本冊 Lesson 7 の英文をもう一度読んで，次の活動に取り組みましょう。

Words and Phrases 英文中に出てきた語句・表現について，それぞれ左側の空所には英語を，右側の空所には日本語の意味を書き入れましょう。

1. Time flies. _____

2. _____ 名 [A1] 娘

3. _____ 副 [A2] 海外へ

4. _____ 名 [A1] 日光

5. reverse 動 [B2] _____

6. hemisphere 名 _____

7. name 動 [B1] _____

8. _____ 名 [A1] 生き物

9. coastal 形 [B1] _____

10. I bet ... _____

Questions 次の問いに英語で答えましょう。

1. According to the email, what does Peter want to do with Adam's family?

_____

2. When is winter in Australia?

_____

3. According to the email, where in Australia can people enjoy snorkeling?

_____

4. What will Peter's and Adam's families probably choose to eat for dinner in Sydney?

_____

Express Yourself あなたが家族と海外旅行に行くとして，訪れる場所や旅行中にしたいことを下の Travel Itinerary（旅程表）のそれぞれの日に 1 〜 2 文程度の英語で書いてみましょう。

Travel Itinerary	
FLIGHT DEPARTURE: Narita Airport	
FLIGHT ARRIVAL: _____	
DAY 1	WHAT TO DO: _____
DAY 2	WHAT TO DO: _____

HINTS 自分が行ってみたい国の情報をインターネットなどを使って調べてみましょう。旅程の内容はそれぞれ We will 〜 で書き始めるとよいでしょう。

Helpful Expressions enjoy seeing a wonderful view「すばらしい景色を見て楽しむ」

本冊 Lesson 8 の英文をもう一度読んで，次の活動に取り組みましょう。

Words and Phrases 英文中に出てきた語句・表現について，それぞれ左側の空所には英語を，右側の空所には日本語の意味を書き入れましょう。

1. term 名 [B1] ....
2. eagerly 副 [B2] ....
3. import 動 [B2] ....
4. innovative 形 [B2] ....
5. origin 名 [B1] ....

6. relative 名 [B1] ....
7. coworker 名 ....
8. region 名 [B1] ....
9. souvenir 名 [B1] ....
10. be derived from ... .

Questions 次の問いに英語で答えましょう。

1. According to the passage, what did Japanese people do in the middle of the sixth century?

....

2. What calendar is used in Japan now?

....

3. Why do many tourists from abroad buy Japanese clay bells as souvenirs?

....

4. What is the only difference between the Japanese zodiac signs and the Chinese ones?

....

Express Yourself 年賀状の挨拶を40〜50語程度の英語で書いてみましょう。

Happy New Year, ... **!**

....
....
....
....

HINTS ALT の先生や友達など，年賀状を送りたい人を思い浮かべて宛先に記入しましょう。「また学校で会えるのを楽しみにしています」といった新学期に向けた挨拶や，新年の抱負などを考えてみましょう。

Helpful Expressions I am looking forward to seeing you at school. 「学校で会えるのを楽しみにしています。」
I wish you a happy New Year. 「充実した一年になりますように。」
My resolution for this year is to 〜. 「今年の抱負は〜することです。」
When the new term starts, ... 「新学期が始まったら…」

本冊 Lesson 9 の英文をもう一度読んで，次の活動に取り組みましょう。

Words and Phrases 英文中に出てきた語句・表現について，それぞれ左側の空所には英語を，右側の空所には日本語の意味を書き入れましょう。

1. advance 動 [B1] ＿＿＿＿＿＿＿＿＿

2. ＿＿＿＿＿＿＿＿＿ 動 [A2] …を発明する

3. match 動 [B1] ＿＿＿＿＿＿＿＿＿

4. as a result ＿＿＿＿＿＿＿＿＿

5. machinery 名 ＿＿＿＿＿＿＿＿＿

6. for fear of … ＿＿＿＿＿＿＿＿＿

7. deprive A of B ＿＿＿＿＿＿＿＿＿

8. eliminate 動 [B1] ＿＿＿＿＿＿＿＿＿

9. typically 副 [B1] ＿＿＿＿＿＿＿＿＿

10. as a matter of course ＿＿＿＿＿＿＿＿＿

Questions 次の問いに英語で答えましょう。

1. According to the passage, why are some people afraid of AI?

＿＿＿＿＿＿＿＿＿＿＿＿＿＿＿＿＿＿＿＿＿＿＿＿＿＿＿＿＿＿＿

2. According to the passage, what made elevator operators unnecessary?

＿＿＿＿＿＿＿＿＿＿＿＿＿＿＿＿＿＿＿＿＿＿＿＿＿＿＿＿＿＿＿

3. What is listed in the report from MIT as one of the new jobs which will appear?

＿＿＿＿＿＿＿＿＿＿＿＿＿＿＿＿＿＿＿＿＿＿＿＿＿＿＿＿＿＿＿

4. According to the passage, what will we become able to do, thanks to AI?

＿＿＿＿＿＿＿＿＿＿＿＿＿＿＿＿＿＿＿＿＿＿＿＿＿＿＿＿＿＿＿

Express Yourself あなたの身のまわりで最新技術や AI が活用されている製品をひとつ選び，その機能などを40〜50語程度の英語で説明してみましょう。

＿＿＿＿＿＿＿＿＿＿＿＿＿＿＿＿＿＿＿＿＿＿＿＿＿＿＿＿＿＿＿

＿＿＿＿＿＿＿＿＿＿＿＿＿＿＿＿＿＿＿＿＿＿＿＿＿＿＿＿＿＿＿

＿＿＿＿＿＿＿＿＿＿＿＿＿＿＿＿＿＿＿＿＿＿＿＿＿＿＿＿＿＿＿

＿＿＿＿＿＿＿＿＿＿＿＿＿＿＿＿＿＿＿＿＿＿＿＿＿＿＿＿＿＿＿

HINTS 身近な製品の例としては「自動運転車」「スマートスピーカー」「掃除ロボット」などがあります。

Helpful Expressions a nursing-care robot「介護ロボット」
a robot vacuum cleaner「ロボット掃除機」
a self-driving car「自動運転車」

本冊 Lesson 10 の英文をもう一度読んで，次の活動に取り組みましょう。

Words and Phrases 英文中に出てきた語句・表現について，それぞれ左側の空所には英語を，右側の空所には日本語の意味を書き入れましょう。

1. get married to ... ﹍﹍﹍﹍﹍﹍﹍﹍

2. all the way ﹍﹍﹍﹍﹍﹍﹍﹍

3. due to ... ﹍﹍﹍﹍﹍﹍﹍﹍

4. ﹍﹍﹍﹍﹍﹍ 形 [A1] (雪などが)ひどい

5. groom 名 [B1] ﹍﹍﹍﹍﹍﹍﹍﹍

6. get together ﹍﹍﹍﹍﹍﹍﹍﹍

7. ﹍﹍﹍﹍﹍ 名 [A2] 新婦

8. live 形 [B1] ﹍﹍﹍﹍﹍﹍﹍﹍

9. ﹍﹍﹍﹍﹍ 名 [A1] 会話

10. see off ... ﹍﹍﹍﹍﹍﹍﹍﹍

Questions 次の問いに英語で答えましょう。

1. According to the passage, when did the writer attend a wedding ceremony in England?

﹍﹍﹍﹍﹍﹍﹍﹍﹍﹍﹍﹍﹍﹍﹍﹍﹍﹍﹍﹍﹍﹍﹍﹍

2. According to the passage, why were all the trains after the writer's train canceled?

﹍﹍﹍﹍﹍﹍﹍﹍﹍﹍﹍﹍﹍﹍﹍﹍﹍﹍﹍﹍﹍﹍﹍﹍

3. What was Hilary probably doing the night before the wedding?

﹍﹍﹍﹍﹍﹍﹍﹍﹍﹍﹍﹍﹍﹍﹍﹍﹍﹍﹍﹍﹍﹍﹍﹍

4. According to the passage, what did the writer do at the end of the last party?

﹍﹍﹍﹍﹍﹍﹍﹍﹍﹍﹍﹍﹍﹍﹍﹍﹍﹍﹍﹍﹍﹍﹍﹍

Express Yourself あなたが海外でしてみたいことを，その理由とともに40〜50語程度の英語で書いてみましょう。

﹍﹍﹍﹍﹍﹍﹍﹍﹍﹍﹍﹍﹍﹍﹍﹍﹍﹍﹍﹍﹍﹍﹍﹍

﹍﹍﹍﹍﹍﹍﹍﹍﹍﹍﹍﹍﹍﹍﹍﹍﹍﹍﹍﹍﹍﹍﹍﹍

﹍﹍﹍﹍﹍﹍﹍﹍﹍﹍﹍﹍﹍﹍﹍﹍﹍﹍﹍﹍﹍﹍﹍﹍

﹍﹍﹍﹍﹍﹍﹍﹍﹍﹍﹍﹍﹍﹍﹍﹍﹍﹍﹍﹍﹍﹍﹍﹍

HINTS 本文のように，日本と海外の違いが楽しめることを考えてみてもおもしろいでしょう。山登りや海水浴など，海外の自然を楽しんだり，日本と海外の両方で展開しているテーマパークに行くことなどが考えられます。

本冊 Lesson 11 の英文をもう一度読んで，次の活動に取り組みましょう。

Words and Phrases 英文中に出てきた語句・表現について，それぞれ左側の空所には英語を，右側の空所には日本語の意味を書き入れましょう。

1. distinguish 動 [B1] ....
2. .... 動 [A2] …を表す
3. convey a message ....
4. generally 副 [B1] ....
5. authority 名 [B1] ....

6. innocence 名 ....
7. recognize 動 [B1] ....
8. rectangle 名 ....
9. horizontally 副 ....
10. interpret 動 [B2] ....

Questions 次の問いに英語で答えましょう。

1. According to the passage, can the colors of flags be communication tools?

....

2. What is the general meaning of the color black?

....

3. What does the yellow circle mean in the Australian Aboriginal flag?

....

4. According to the passage, why is red not used in the flag of the United Nations?

....

Express Yourself 次の質問について，あなたの考えを理由とともに40〜50語程度の英語で書いてみましょう。

Question: What color do you most like to wear?

....

....

....

....

HINTS あなたはどんな色の服が好きでしょうか。理由としては，「シンプルだから黒色が好き」や「好きな芸能人が着ているからピンク色が好き」などが考えられます。

本冊 Lesson 12 の英文をもう一度読んで，次の活動に取り組みましょう。

Words and Phrases
英文中に出てきた語句・表現について，それぞれ左側の空所には英語を，右側の空所には日本語の意味を書き入れましょう。

1. currency 名 [B1] _____
2. determine 動 [B1] _____
3. ratio 名 _____
4. _____ 動 [A2] …を比較する
5. in theory _____

6. _____ 名 [A2] 広告
7. export 動 [B2] _____
8. consumption 名 [B1] _____
9. relative 形 [B1] _____
10. take ... into account _____

Questions
次の問いに英語で答えましょう。

1. According to the first article, what is purchasing power parity?

_____

_____

2. According to the first article, what is the Big Mac index used for?

_____

3. According to the graph, how many times as expensive is a Big Mac in Switzerland than in Russia?

_____

4. What does Y. T. think will affect the total price of a Big Mac?

_____

_____

Express Yourself
次の質問について，あなたの考えを理由とともに40～50語程度の英語で書いてみましょう。

Question: Which do you prefer, shopping online or purchasing at a local store?

_____

_____

_____

_____

HINTS オンラインショッピングは便利さや手軽さが主なメリットです。地元の店で買い物をするのは商品をすぐに持って帰ることができることが主なメリットです。これらを参考にして自分の意見を考えてみましょう。

Helpful Expressions
fresh food「生鮮食品」
place an order online「オンラインで注文をする」
rot [go bad]「（食品が）腐る」
store hours「営業時間」

本冊 Lesson 13 の英文をもう一度読んで，次の活動に取り組みましょう。

Words and Phrases 英文中に出てきた語句・表現について，それぞれ左側の空所には英語を，右側の空所には日本語の意味を書き入れましょう。

1. freshman 图 [B1] ....
2. responsibility 图 [B1] ....
3. turn A into B ....
4. .... 形 [A2] 自信がある
5. attentive 形 [B2] ....

6. be in charge of ... .
7. realization 图 [B2] ....
8. .... 動 [A2] …を励ます
9. behave 動 [B1] ....
10. enthusiastically 副 [B2] ....

Questions 次の問いに英語で答えましょう。

1. When was Oliver chosen as a volunteer English teacher?

....

2. What did Alonso think about class at first?

....

....

3. What did Oliver find out while teaching his students?

....

4. According to the postcard, how does Alonso feel toward Oliver?

....

Express Yourself あなたにとって「よい先生」とはどのような先生ですか。書き出しに続けて合計40〜50語程度の英語で書いてみましょう。

Good teachers ....

....

....

....

HINTS 本冊 Lesson 13 の本文の内容も参考になるでしょう。

Helpful Expressions be strict with ... 「…に対して厳しい」
be tolerant of mistakes 「失敗に寛容である」
pay careful attention to ... 「…に対して注意深く気を配る」
spoil ... 「…を甘やかす」

本冊 Lesson 14 の英文をもう一度読んで，次の活動に取り組みましょう。

Words and Phrases 英文中に出てきた語句・表現について，それぞれ左側の空所には英語を，右側の空所には日本語の意味を書き入れましょう。

1. socialize 動 [B2] ....
2. take ... for granted ....
3. integrated 形 ....
4. .... 名 [A2] 電球
5. leap 名 [B2] ....

6. appliance 名 ....
7. cut down ... .
8. adaptive 形 ....
9. become aware of ... .
10. as time goes by ....

Questions 次の問いに英語で答えましょう。

1. According to the passage, in what way were the 1980s different from the present?

....

2. According to the passage, what can people do with a smart light bulb?

....

3. According to the passage, why can smart thermostats save money?

....

....

4. According to the passage, what does home automation offer us?

....

Express Yourself 次の表を参考に，自分が使ってみたいスマート家電を，その理由とともに40〜50語程度の英語で書いてみましょう。

....

....

....

....

Smart Home Appliances	
1. Intelligent Oven	2. Automatic Feeder
This modern oven can automatically recognize the food in the oven and show you the best recipe. You can see the inside of the oven and control the temperature by using your smartphone.	This feeder can feed your pet automatically, and it provides you with a nutritional analysis of your pet. You can also see if your pet is OK through the camera on the feeder when you are out.

HINTS 自分はどう活用するかを考え，I would like to use ... から文を始めてみましょう。feeder は「エサやり機」という意味。

Helpful Expressions it is useful for 〜ing ...「それは…を〜するのに役立ちます」

本冊 Lesson 15 の英文をもう一度読んで，次の活動に取り組みましょう。

Words and Phrases 英文中に出てきた語句・表現について，それぞれ左側の空所には英語を，右側の空所には日本語の意味を書き入れましょう。

1. essential 形 [B1] ....
2. .... 動 [A2] …を出版する
3. think of ... .
4. rapidly 副 [B1] ....
5. widespread 形 [B1] ....

6. mention 動 [B1] ....
7. popularity 名 [B2] ....
8. .... 名 [A2] 世代
9. expand 動 [B1] ....
10. .... 名 [A2] 市場

Questions 次の問いに英語で答えましょう。

1. According to the passage, when was the word "manga" first used?

....

2. According to the passage, what is Tezuaka Osamu regarded as?

....

....

3. Where is Astro Boy used?

....

4. What can people do at manga cafés?

....

Express Yourself あなたのお気に入りの漫画の紹介文を，40〜50語程度の英語で書いてみましょう。

My favorite manga : ....

....

....

....

....

HINTS Lesson 3 同様に，紹介文を読んだ人がその漫画を読みたくなるような文を書きましょう。

Helpful Expressions I would like to introduce ... 「…を紹介したいと思います」
recommend 「…を薦める」
The story goes this way. ... 「ストーリーは以下のように進んでいきます。…」

本冊 Lesson 16 の英文をもう一度読んで，次の活動に取り組みましょう。

Words and Phrases
英文中に出てきた語句・表現について，それぞれ左側の空所には英語を，右側の空所には日本語の意味を書き入れましょう。

1. nutrition 图 [B1] _____
2. prove 動 [B1] _____
3. irrelevant 形 _____
4. for the sake of ... _____
5. fight against ... _____

6. deficiency 图 [B1] _____
7. approximately 副 [B1] _____
8. maintain 動 [B1] _____
9. restrict 動 [B1] _____
10. in the long run _____

Questions
次の問いに英語で答えましょう。

1. What did Mark try to disprove?

_____

_____

2. During his Twinkie diet, what did Mark eat other than junk foods?

_____

3. By the end of the diet, Mark was able to lose 27 pounds.　What happened to the amount of his body fat?

_____

4. Does the writer think the Twinkie diet is reliable?　Why or why not?

_____

_____

Express Yourself
下の表に，それぞれ30語程度の英語を書き入れましょう。

Junk Foods and Healthy Alternatives
You want to avoid eating some junk foods because they are too fatty or too high in calories.　What kind of healthy alternatives would you recommend instead of these junk foods?

Hamburgers	
Hamburgers	
Coke	

HINTS　左に示されたジャンクフードの代わりにおすすめしたいものを，I would like to recommend ... などで始まる文で書いてみましょう。

Helpful Expressions　fatty「脂肪の多い」　　prevent diseases「病気を防ぐ」

本冊 Lesson 17 の英文をもう一度読んで，次の活動に取り組みましょう。

Words and Phrases 英文中に出てきた語句・表現について，それぞれ左側の空所には英語を，右側の空所には日本語の意味を書き入れましょう。

1. contrary to ...　_____

2. a number of ...　_____

3. _____ 名 [A2] 事故

4. come to mind　_____

5. associate A with B　_____

6. burden 名 [B1]　_____

7. exhausted 形 [B1]　_____

8. promote 動 [B1]　_____

9. safety 名 [B1]　_____

10. at the moment　_____

Questions 次の問いに英語で答えましょう。

1. According to Graph 2, in which country are self-driving cars most likely to be popular?

_____

2. According to Chris' report, how would freight drivers not feel if they used self-driving cars?

_____

3. According to Kazuma's report, why is it unlikely that self-driving cars will become usual soon in Japan?

_____

4. Why is a human driver needed in order to use a self-driving car in Japan?

_____

_____

Express Yourself 次の質問について，あなたの考えを理由とともに40～50語程度の英語で書いてみましょう。

Question：Will self-driving cars become usual in Japan?

_____

_____

_____

_____

HINTS 本冊 Lesson 17 のグラフや本文を参考に自動運転車のメリットやデメリットを考えてみましょう。

Helpful Expressions affordable「購入しやすい，入手可能な」
be more [less] likely to ～「～する可能性が高い[低い]」
the traffic infrastructure「交通インフラ」

本冊 Lesson 18 の英文をもう一度読んで，次の活動に取り組みましょう。

Words and Phrases　英文中に出てきた語句・表現について，それぞれ左側の空所には英語を，右側の空所には日本語の意味を書き入れましょう。

1. decade 名 [B2]　.............................

2. textile 名　.............................

3. be in short supply　.............................

4. withdraw 動 [B2]　.............................

5. contract 名 [B2]　.............................

6. discard 動　.............................

7. ....　動 [A2] …を縫う

8. be dependent upon ...　.............................

9. launch 動 [B1]　.............................

10. meanwhile 副 [B1]　.............................

Questions　次の問いに英語で答えましょう。

1. According to the passage, what company most contributed to making Okayama a denim mecca?

....

2. According to the passage, why did Maruo leave the school uniform business?

....

....

3. According to the passage, what did Maruo do by using B-grade rolls of denim?

....

4. Why was the "Kojima Jeans Street" planned?

....

Express Yourself　自分が住んでいる地域や行ってみたい観光地の歴史について知っていることや調べたことを，40〜50語程度の英語で書いてみましょう。

Place: ....

....

....

....

....

HINTS　たくさんのことを細かく書くのではなく，大まかな流れを書くようにするとよいでしょう。

Helpful Expressions　be established as ... 「…として制定される」

be known as ... 「…として知られている」

be located in ... 「…に位置する」

本冊 Lesson 19 の英文をもう一度読んで，次の活動に取り組みましょう。

Words and Phrases 英文中に出てきた語句・表現について，それぞれ左側の空所には英語を，右側の空所には日本語の意味を書き入れましょう。

1. evident 形 [B1] ....

2. consist of ... .

3. depression 名 [B1] ....

4. anxiety 名 [B1] ....

5. emotional 形 [B1] ....

6. .... 形 [A2] 軍の

7. make use of ... .

8. in short ....

9. stimulate 動 [B2] ....

10. trait 名 [B2] ....

Questions 次の問いに英語で答えましょう。

1. According to the passage, why is music used as a medical treatment?

....

2. According to the passage, what is music therapy used for in addition to promoting mental and emotional health?

....

3. According to the passage, in what point is the brain the same as other organs?

....
....

4. As a general rule, what kind of music should we listen to when we want to relax?

....

Express Yourself 次の質問について，あなたの考えを理由とともに40～50語程度の英語で書いてみましょう。

Question: What kind of music do you listen to when you feel sad?

....
....
....
....

Helpful Expressions ballad music「バラード音楽」
soothe one's feelings「気分をなだめる」
the lyrics of the song「歌の歌詞」

本冊 Lesson 20 の英文をもう一度読んで，次の活動に取り組みましょう。

Words and Phrases

英文中に出てきた語句・表現について，それぞれ左側の空所には英語を，右側の空所には日本語の意味を書き入れましょう。

1. edible 形 ....   6. surplus 形 ....

2. contribute to ... .   7. poverty 名 [B1] ....

3. starvation 名 [B2] ....   8. legally 副 [B1] ....

4. have nothing to do with ... .   9. indispensable 形 [B2] ....

5. conservative 形 [B1] ....   10. sustainably 副 ....

Questions

次の問いに英語で答えましょう。

1. According to the article, why is it a shame to throw away food you can still eat?

....

2. According to the article, why do Americans throw away billions of pounds of food every year?

....

3. According to the article, what social problems can "food sharing" help to solve?

....

4. According to the article, what law was established in France?

....

....

Express Yourself

食べ物の無駄を減らすアプリを開発したいと思います。そのアプリの機能を考え，書き出しに続けて合計40〜50語程度の英語で書いてみましょう。

I want to develop an app ....

....

....

....

....

HINTS   connect local farmers directly with consumers「地元農家と消費者を直接つなぐ」
connect people with local supermarkets「人々と地元のスーパーマーケットをつなぐ」
donate unsold food items「売れ残りの食品を寄付する」　food expiration reminders「賞味期限リマインダー」
share surplus food「余剰食品を共有する」　food that has passed its best-before date「賞味期限が切れた食品」

Helpful Expressions   an app that enables us to ～「～することを可能にするアプリ」

解答・解説

Lesson 1

Words and Phrases

1. international　　2. ～することが予想される
3. …を専攻する　　4. …を登録する　　5. 前の
6. trade　　7. 産業　　8. 文学
9. 遠慮なく～する　　10. 学部学生

Questions

1. It is for the university students (of Daiichi University).

解説 質問文は「この通知はだれに向けたものか」である。ティーチングアシスタントを募集する大学のウェブサイトなので，この通知のターゲットは大学生である。

2. They are interested in Global Studies.

解説 質問文は「このイベントでインターナショナルハイスクールの生徒の多くは何に興味を持っているか」である。第1段落3文目に注目すると，今回のプログラムに参加する高校生が興味を持っているのはグローバルスタディーズである。

3. They will have it on August 15th.

解説 質問文は「高校生たちは『世界の文学』に関する講義をいつ受けるのか」である。Program Schedule から該当箇所をさがす。On August 15th. でもよい。

4. The professors of the department will.

解説 質問文は「だれがイベント中の講義をする予定か」である。本文20行目に注目する。解答の the department は Global Studies department としてもよい。

Express Yourself

例：High school students are open to new concepts. Working with them will be of value to me. In addition, my background knowledge about global economics will be helpful for students who want to learn what Global Studies is like. （39 words）

和訳 高校生は新しい考え方に対して柔軟です。彼らといっしょに活動することは私にとって価値のあることになります。加えて，世界経済についての私の背景知識は，グローバルスタディーズがどのようなものかを学びたい生徒に役立つでしょう。

Lesson 2

Words and Phrases

1. ～してうれしい　　2. collect　　3. fee
4. ごみ　　5. …を捨てる　　6. 傷んでいる
7. …を寄付する　　8. …を印刷する
9. 必ず～する　　10. …に署名する

Questions

1. It will be held from September 21 to 23.

解説 質問文は「エンドレスサマーフェスティバルの最初のイベントはいつ開かれるか」である。第1段落の5文目に The first one ... will be held from September 21 to 23. とある。

2. They can buy old clothes at reasonable prices.

解説 質問文は「2番目のイベントでは人々は何ができるか」である。第1段落の6文目に The second one is for people who want to buy the clothes at reasonable prices. とある。

3. It started in 2013.

解説 質問文は「エンドレスサマーフェスティバルはいつ始まったか」である。第2段落の1文目の We first started this festival in 2013. に注目する。

4. They will make new clothes from them.

解説 質問文は「古着をエンドレスサマーフェスティバルに寄付した場合，それらを使ってエンドレスサマーは何をするか」である。第2段落の7・8文目の If your clothes are too worn out or too old to sell, you can donate them as well. We can make new clothes from them. に注目する。主語は It としてもよい。

Express Yourself

例：I would like to support this environmentally-friendly festival by providing clothes that I no longer need. I can contribute to protecting our environment through this activity. （26 words）

和訳 私はもう必要のない服を提供することで，この環境にやさしいフェスティバルを応援したいです。私はこの活動をとおして私たちの環境を守ることに貢献できます。

Lesson 3

Words and Phrases

1. award　　2. …によって計画される　　3. 機会
4. 恋に落ちる　　5. explore　　6. 観点
7. stuff　　8. 客観的な　　9. …を行う
10. …と関係がある

Questions

1. It officially started on November 22, 1996.

解説 質問文は「レオナルド図書館大賞はいつ公式に始まったか」である。ポスター上部の説明の中の The award officially started ... の情報を読み取る。

2. We can listen to special talks by the authors of the top three books (of the year).

解説 質問文は「この年のイベントで何を聞くことができるか」である。"Announcement of

Special Interviews" の説明中から「上位 3 冊の著者が招待されること」,「その著者の特別講話を聞けること」を読み取る。

3. Andrew Willy is.

解説 質問文は「おそらく本の読み方についての話をするのはだれか」である。明確には示されていないが,それぞれの本の内容から,本の読み方について話しそうな作家を推測する。

4. It will take place in Leonard Library Room 504.

解説 質問文は「そのイベントはどこで行われるか」である。このイベントの日時と場所について述べているところに注目するとよい。take place「起こる,行われる」

Express Yourself

例：My Favorite Book: *Homo Deus*
The book I would like to share with you is *Homo Deus* by Yuval Noah Harari. According to the author, human beings will evolve into Homo Deus and overcome a lot of difficulties we are facing now. If you want to know about your future, you should read this book. （50 words）

和訳 私が共有したい本はユヴァル・ノア・ハラリの『ホモ・デウス』という本です。筆者によると,人類はホモ・デウスに進化し,現在直面しているたくさんの困難を克服するだろうということです。もし自分の未来のことについて知りたいのならば,この本を読むとよいでしょう。

Lesson 4

Words and Phrases

1. …を利用できる　　2. …について心配する
3. かなりの　　4. budget　　5. …を保持する
6. …に夢中になる　　7. ～するよう誘惑される
8. personal　　9. …に固執する
10. education

Questions

1. They are considering introducing tablet computers into their classes (in order to replace textbooks).

解説 質問文は「日本の一部の学校は何を検討しているか」である。第 1 段落 3 文目に,Some schools in Japan are considering introducing tablet computers into their classes in order to replace textbooks. とある。

2. Because they need to attend them to learn how to use the tablets and software packages.

解説 質問文は「タブレットパソコンを学校に導入した後,なぜ教員たちが研修プログラムに参加す

る必要があるのか」である。1. This will cost a lot of money. の 3 文目の Also, teachers need to attend training programs to learn how to use the tablets and software packages. を参考にする。

3. Because they read digital textbooks more slowly.

別解：Because they can understand and retain the information in them more efficiently.

解説 質問文は「なぜソフィアは生徒が紙の教科書を読むべきだと思っているのか」である。2. Reading is slower with digital text. の内容から答えを作る。解答のように「デジタル教科書のほうが読むのが遅くなる」と,デジタル教科書のデメリットを述べてもよいが,別解のように「紙の教科書のほうが,情報をより効率的に理解し保持できる」と,紙の教科書のメリットを述べてもよい。

4. He calls them old-fashioned.

解説 質問文は「タブレットパソコンやデジタル教科書を使わない教育方式をダニエルは何と呼んでいるか」である。ダニエルのコメントから,タブレット等を使用する授業とどう対比されているか読み取る。

Express Yourself

例：The biggest advantage of introducing tablet computers into the classroom is that it is good for the environment. Since students can read their study materials on their tablets, schools can save a lot of paper by not giving out paper handouts. （41 words）

和訳 タブレットパソコンを教室に導入する最大の利点は,環境によいことです。生徒は自分のタブレット上で教材を読むことができるので,学校は紙の資料を配らないことによって多くの紙を節約することができます。

Lesson 5

Words and Phrases

1. …に分類される　　2. …の危機にある
3. reveal　　4. …を捕らえる　　5. …を思いつく
6. 全体の　　7. …の跡を追う　　8. 移動,移住
9. 破壊　　10. 生息地

Questions

1. There are seven species (of them in the world).

解説 質問文は「世界にはウミガメが何種類いるか」である。本文冒頭に,There are seven species of sea turtles worldwide. とある。

2. They swim thousands of miles to lay eggs on the same tiny island where their mothers laid

their eggs.

解説 質問文は「なぜ一部の種のウミガメは生涯に数千マイルも泳ぐのか」である。第2段落2文目の「〜するために」を表すto-不定詞以下が，ウミガメが数千マイルを移動する目的を表している。

3. He used [tracked her by using] satellite tracking technology.

解説 質問文は「ウォレス・J・ニコルズはどのようにしてアデリータを追跡したか」である。第3段落4文目の，... by using satellite tracking technology. が答えとなる。

4. They shared Adelita's travel around the ocean (on the Internet).

解説 質問文は「何百万人もの子供たちがインターネットを使って何をしたか」である。第4段落3文目の ..., but millions of kids shared her travel around the ocean on the Internet. から答えを作る。

Express Yourself

例：We throw away a huge amount of waste into the ocean, and this causes sea water pollution. This is one of the reasons why some marine animals are in danger of extinction. If we reduce our waste and make the ocean cleaner, we can save them. (46 words)

和訳 私たちはばく大な量のごみを海に捨てており，このことが海洋汚染を引き起こしています。これが一部の海洋生物が絶滅の危機に瀕している理由のひとつです。もし私たちがごみを減らし，海をきれいにすれば，彼らを救うことができます。

Lesson 6

Words and Phrases

1. pollution　　2. 現在の　　3. …を消費する
4. convenience　　5. …に対処する
6. 問題(点)　　7. 禁止(令)
8. (法律などが)発効される
9. …を供給する　　10. 制限

Questions

1. Plastic pollution in the ocean is.

解説 質問文は「琢朗の文章によれば，世界で大きな問題となっているのは何か」である。第1段落1文目に Plastic pollution in the ocean is becoming a big problem around the world. とあり，これが答えとなる。

2. It is to show consumers how important it is to reduce plastic waste.

解説 質問文は「記事中で示された活動の主な目的は何か」である。The main purpose of this

action を It で受けて答えを作る。

3. They call for further restrictions on other single-use items.

解説 質問文は「アドガー教授の返信によれば，環境保護論者が求めているものは何か」である。Environmentalists have ... called for further restrictions on other single-use items. とある。

4. They are going to have a debate session.

解説 質問文は「琢朗たちは次のアドガー教授の授業で何をする予定か」である。アドガー教授の返信に，We would like to have a debate session ... とある。

Express Yourself

例：In my opinion, we should avoid using plastic products, such as plastic bags and plastic straws. Plastic waste remains in the ocean and will not decompose. Therefore, the first thing we should do is reduce our use of plastic products. (40 words)

和訳 私の意見では，ビニール袋やプラスチック製ストローといったプラスチック製品を使うのを避けるべきです。プラスチックごみは海に残り続け，分解されません。そのため，私たちが第一にすべきことは，プラスチック製品の使用を減らすことです。

Lesson 7

Words and Phrases

1. あっという間だ。(光陰矢の如し)　　2. daughter
3. overseas　　4. sunshine
5. …を反対にする　　6. 半球　　7. …を選ぶ
8. life　　9. 沿岸の　　10. きっと…だ

Questions

1. He wants to travel to Australia this winter with them.

解説 質問文は「ピーターはアダム一家と何をしたいか」である。第2段落2・3文目を参考に答えを作る。Would you like to join us? は「ごいっしょにどうですか」と相手を誘うときによく使う表現。

2. It is from June to August.

解説 質問文は「オーストラリアの冬はいつか」である。第2段落6文目に Winter in Australia is from June to August ... とある。

3. They can enjoy it at Manly Beach (in Sydney).

解説 質問文は「オーストラリアのどこでシュノーケリングを楽しむことができるか」である。第3段落3文目に，Snorkeling is the most popular activity there. とあり，there は Manly Beach

のことである。

4. They will probably choose seafood.

解説 質問文は「ピーターとアダムの家族はシドニーでの夕食におそらく何を選ぶか」である。メールの最後でピーターが, ..., we should try the seafood there! と強く提案しているので, シーフードを選ぶことが推測される。

Express Yourself

例・和訳：FLIGHT ARRIVAL：Sydney Airport

DAY 1：We will go to Manly Beach in Sydney and see some of the unique marine life of Australia by snorkeling. （シドニーのマンリービーチに行って, シュノーケリングをしてオーストラリア独自の海の生き物を見ます。）

DAY 2：We will rent a bike and enjoy seeing beautiful coastal views by bike. After that, we will go to an Australian local restaurant and enjoy seafood there. （自転車をレンタルして, 自転車で美しい沿岸の景色を見て楽しみます。そのあと, オーストラリアの地元のレストランに行って, そこでシーフードを楽しみます。）

Lesson 8

Words and Phrases

1. 専門用語　　2. 熱心に　　3. …を輸入する
4. 革新的な　　5. 起源　　6. 親戚, 親類
7. 同僚　　8. 地域　　9. 土産
10. …に由来する

Questions

1. They eagerly imported innovative ideas and systems from China.

解説 質問文は「6世紀半ばの日本人は何をしたか」である。第1段落3文目の, When Buddhism arrived in Japan in the middle of the sixth century, ... 以下の内容に注目する。

2. The Gregorian calendar is.

解説 質問文は「日本では今どの暦が使われているか」である。第2段落冒頭に In modern times, Japan uses the Gregorian calendar, ... とある。in modern times は「現代では」という意味。

3. Because they are not very expensive.

解説 質問文は「なぜ多くの外国人旅行者は日本の土鈴を土産に買うのか」である。第3段落最後に Since they are not very expensive, ... とある。since が理由を表す接続詞として使われていることがポイントとなる。

4. It is that the last animal is a boar in Japan, but a pig in China.

解説 質問文は「日本の干支と中国の干支の唯一の違いは何か」である。第4段落2文目に The only difference is that the last animal is a boar in Japan, but a pig in China. とあり, これがそのまま答えとなる。

Express Yourself

例：One year has passed, and another year has come. I wish you a wonderful New Year with the hope that it will be filled with happiness and delight. I am looking forward to seeing you at school when the new term starts. （42 words）

和訳 1年が終わり, また新たな1年がやってきました。幸せと喜びに包まれた希望とともに, すばらしい一年になることを願っています。新学期が始まったら学校であなたに会えるのを楽しみにしています。

Lesson 9

Words and Phrases

1. 進歩する　　2. invent　　3. …に匹敵する
4. 結果として　　5. 機械　　6. …を恐れて
7. AからBを奪う　　8. …を除く　　9. 一般的に
10. 当然のこととして

Questions

1. Because they think (that) it will take a lot of jobs away from human beings.

解説 質問文は「なぜ AI を恐れる人々がいるのか」である。第1段落2文目の ..., and others are afraid that it (＝AI) will take a lot of jobs away from human beings. を参考に答えを作る。

2. The automation of elevators did. [Automatic elevators did.]

解説 質問文は「何がエレベーターのオペレーターを不必要にしたか」である。第2段落最終文に注目する。質問文に合うように, 「エレベーターの自動化」がオペレーターを不要にしたと考えて, automation「自動化」という名詞を使うとよい。また, automatic「自動の」という形容詞を使って, Automatic elevators did. としてもよい。

3. The job of "empathy trainer" (for AI devices) is.

解説 質問文は「これから現れる新しい仕事のひとつとして何が MIT の報告書にあげられているか」である。第4段落3文目に, The report lists new jobs, like that of "empathy trainer" for AI devices. とある。

4. We will become able to focus on more complex and creative tasks.

解説 質問文は「AI のおかげで, 私たちは何ができるようになるか」である。最終文に注目すると, AI や新技術のおかげで人間ができるようになる

ことが示されている。

Express Yourself

例：I have a robot vacuum cleaner which automatically moves around and cleans a room. The sensors on it detect the distance to an obstacle and control the speed. In addition, it returns to the charger automatically when the battery level is low. (42 words)

和訳 私は自動的に動き回って部屋を掃除するロボット掃除機を持っています。掃除機についているセンサーは障害物との距離を検知し，速度を制御します。さらに，電池残量が少なくなると，それは自動的に充電器に戻ります。

Lesson 10

Words and Phrases

1. …と結婚する　2. はるばる　3. …のために
4. heavy　5. 新郎　6. 集まる　7. bride
8. 生の　9. conversation　10. …を見送る

Questions

1. He attended it on March 3, 2018.

解説 質問文は「筆者はいつイギリスで結婚式に参列したか」である。第1段落1文目に注目する。

2. They were canceled due to the heavy snow.

解説 質問文は「なぜ筆者の乗った列車以降の列車はすべて運休になったのか」である。第2段落3文目を参考に答えを作る。

3. She was probably enjoying a party with her (same-sex) friends.

解説 質問文は「ヒラリーは結婚式の前夜におそらく何をしていたか」である。第3段落最終文の，..., a party of the same kind was held for the bride in another place. から，新婦であるヒラリーも同性の友人とパーティーをしていたことが推測される。

4. He saw off the bride and groom as they left for their honeymoon.

解説 質問文は「筆者は最後のパーティーの終わりに何をしたか」である。第5段落最終文を参考に答えを作る。

Express Yourself

例：I would like to go mountain climbing in a foreign country. I have climbed Mt. Fuji, but I would like to try to climb a higher mountain such as Mt. Everest. I want to enjoy different views from what I have seen from the tops of mountains in Japan. (49 words)

和訳 私は外国で登山に行きたいです。私は富士山に登ったことがありますが，エベレストのような

さらに高い山に登ってみたいです。私は日本の山の頂上から見た景色とは違った景色を楽しみたいのです。

Lesson 11

Words and Phrases

1. …を区別する　2. represent
3. メッセージを伝える　4. 一般的に　5. 権威
6. 無罪，無邪気　7. …を認める　8. 長方形
9. 水平に　10. …を解釈する

Questions

1. Yes, they can.

解説 質問文は「旗の色はコミュニケーションツールになりうるか」である。第1段落最終文に，..., the colors convey certain messages to us. とあり，これは色がコミュニケーションのために使われていることを示している。

2. It is power and authority.

解説 質問文は「黒色の一般的な意味は何か」である。第2段落2文目に，黒色と白色の一般的な意味が述べられている。

3. It means the sun.

解説 質問文は「オーストラリアのアボリジニの旗で黄色の円は何を意味するか」である。第3段落最終文で，アボリジニの旗のそれぞれの色が何を意味するかが述べられている。

4. Because red may remind people (in other countries) of blood or wars.

解説 質問文は「赤色が国連の旗に使われないのはなぜか」である。第4段落最終文に，Some people say that is why red is not used ... とあるので，直前の文に理由が述べられているとわかる。

Express Yourself

例：I like to wear blue, because I feel confident and strong when I wear blue. That's why I have many blue shirts and skirts. In addition, I like Queen Elsa in the Disney movie "Frozen." She always wears a blue dress and I really feel sympathetic toward her. (48 words)

和訳 私は青色を身につけるのが好きです。なぜなら，青色を着ると自信がわいて強くなったように感じるからです。だから，私はたくさんの青色のシャツやスカートを持っています。加えて，私はディズニー映画『アナと雪の女王』のエルサ女王が好きです。彼女はいつも青いドレスを着ていて，私は彼女にとても共感します。

Lesson 12

Words and Phrases

1. 通貨　　2. …を決定する　　3. 比率
4. compare　　5. 理論上は　　6. advertising
7. …を輸出する　　8. 消費　　9. 相対的な
10. …を考慮する

Questions

1. It is an economic theory which states that the currency exchange rate can be determined by the ratio of the purchasing power between two currencies.

解説 質問文は「購買力平価とは何か」である。第1段落1文目を参考に答えを作る。

2. It is used for comparing the values of currencies.

解説 質問文は「ビッグマック指数は何のために使われるか」である。第1段落最終文を参考に答えを作る。It is used to compare the values of currencies. としてもよい。

3. It is about three times as expensive.

解説 質問文は「スイスではビッグマックがロシアより何倍高価か」である。グラフを見るとスイスのビッグマックの値段は6.71ドルで，ロシアのビッグマックの値段は2.2ドルである。およそ3倍の違いがある。これについて倍数表現を使って表す。

4. He [She] thinks tariff rates, consumption tax rates, and the economic condition of each country will.

解説 質問文は「Y. T. は何がビッグマックの総額に影響すると考えているか」である。Y. T. による意見の，The total price of ... で始まる文を参考にする。本文では受動態で記述されているが，質問に合わせて能動態で解答したい。

Express Yourself

例：I prefer shopping online because it is more convenient than purchasing at a local store. With online shopping, I can place orders whenever I need to without worrying about the store hours and the holidays of the store. It saves me a lot of time and effort. (47 words)

別解：I prefer shopping at a local store, especially when I buy fresh foods. It is hard to buy fresh fish or fruits online because they may rot during transportation. If we buy them at a local store, we can enjoy them fresh. (42 words)

和訳 地元の店で買い物をするより便利なので，オンラインで買うほうを好みます。オンラインショッピングでは，店の営業時間や休日のことを気にすることなくいつでも必要なときに注文ができます。それは私の時間と労力を削減してくれます。

別解：特に生鮮食品を買うときについては，地元の店で買うのを好みます。新鮮な魚や果物をオンラインで購入するのは難しいです。なぜなら，それらは輸送中に腐ってしまうかもしれないからです。もし地元の店でそれらを買えば，食品を新鮮な状態で楽しむことができます。

Lesson 13

Words and Phrases

1. (大学の)新入生，1年生　　2. 責任
3. AをBに変える　　4. confident
5. 注意深い　　6. …を担当している
7. 認識，理解　　8. encourage　　9. ふるまう
10. 熱心に

Questions

1. He was chosen as one in the summer after his freshman year of university.

解説 質問文は「オリバーはいつボランティアの英語教員に選ばれたか」である。第1段落1文目に注目する。

2. He thought class was a good time to train his basketball skills (by tossing plastic bottles into the trash can from his desk).

解説 質問文は「アロンソは最初，授業のことをどのように思っていたか」である。第2段落1文目を参考に答えを作る。質問文の at first は「最初は」という意味で，その後は違うということを示唆する。

3. He found out that even teachers have much to learn.

解説 質問文は「生徒に教えながらオリバーがわかったことは何か」である。第4段落最後の2文に注目する。I once thought ... 「かつて…だと思っていた」に続いて，However, ... とあるので，However に続く内容が今回オリバーがわかったことである。

4. He feels sorry for the way he behaved at the camp.

解説 質問文は「アロンソはオリバーに対してどう感じているか」である。はがきの1文目に注目して解答する。I realized how much fun learning English was ... とあることから，He feels gratitude for Oliver teaching him English enthusiastically.「彼はオリバーに熱心に英語を教えてくれたことを感謝している」としてもよいだろう。

Express Yourself

例：Good teachers always pay attention to their students and try to find out what they really need, but they never spoil their students. Also, they don't hesitate to answer the questions from their students. They should be knowledgeable about their subjects. (41 words)

和訳 よい先生とは常に生徒に気を配り，彼らが本当に必要なものを見つけようとしますが，けっして生徒を甘やかすことはありません。また，彼らは生徒からの質問に答えることをためらいません。彼らが教える教科についてよく知っている必要があります。

Lesson 14

Words and Phrases

1. 打ち解けて交際する
2. …を当然のことだと思う　　3. 統合した
4. bulb　　5. 飛躍　　6. 設備
7. …を削減する　　8. 順応できる
9. …に気づく　　10. 時間がたつにつれて

Questions

1. People used public pay phones in the 1980s.

解説 質問文は「1980年代は現在とどのように異なったか」である。1980年代は人々が公衆電話を使っており，それに対して筆者は It was like a different world! とたとえている。

2. They can turn the light on and off with an app on their smartphones.

解説 質問文は「スマート電球を使って人々は何ができるか」である。第3段落の2文目の if you use a smart light bulb, … に続く箇所を参考にして答えを作る。

3. Because they can control the temperature precisely and they only heat and cool the areas that are being used.

解説 質問文は「なぜスマート温度調節器はお金を節約できるか」である。第4段落の2・3文目に注目する。2文目で，Heating and cooling costs will be cut down if … とあり，質問文では save money で表現されている。3文目がその理由となる。

4. It offers us both improved energy efficiency and broader functionality at home.

解説 質問文は「ホームオートメーションは私たちに何を提供してくれるか」である。第5段落の1文目を参考に答えを作る。

Express Yourself

例：I would like to use the "Automatic Feeder" because it will ease my concerns about my pet dog. Since my family is not at home during the daytime on weekdays, it would be really helpful for us to be able to see our dog with the camera. (47 words)

和訳 私はペットの犬についての心配を解消してくれるので，「自動エサやり機」を使いたいです。私の家族は平日の日中は家にいないので，カメラで犬を見ることができるのはとても助かります。

Lesson 15

Words and Phrases

1. 不可欠の　　2. publish
3. …のことを考える　　4. 急速に
5. 広く普及した　　6. …に言及する
7. 人気　　8. generation　　9. …を拡大する
10. market

Questions

1. It was used late in the 18th century.

解説 質問文は「『漫画』という語はいつ最初に使われたか」である。第2段落1文目を参考に答えを作る。

2. He is regarded as "the god of manga" (for his role in the development of what are now known as story manga).

解説 質問文は「手塚治虫は何とみなされているか」である。第4段落2文目を参考に，設問文に合わせて regarded as … を使って答えを作る。

3. He is used in T-shirts, key rings, bags, posters and thousands of other goods.

解説 質問文は「鉄腕アトムはどこで利用されているか」である。第4段落の，Even today, … の文に注目して解答する。

4. They can read many shelves of manga of various genres in a quiet space for an hourly fee.

解説 質問文は「漫画喫茶で何ができるか」である。第5段落最終文を参考に答えを作る。

Express Yourself

例：My favorite manga: *Detective Conan* (*Meitantei Conan*)

My favorite manga is *Detective Conan*. Do you know the title of the English version of the manga? It is *Case Closed*. If you say, "The case is closed," it means that all the problems of the case are solved. The manga is a long-seller and I cannot wait for the next one to come out. (56 words)

和訳 私の好きな漫画は『名探偵コナン』です。その漫画の英語版タイトルを知っていますか。『ケ

ースクローズド』です。もし "The case is closed" と言うと，その事件のすべての問題が解決したことを意味します。この漫画はロングセラーで，私は次の刊行が待ちきれません。

Lesson 16

Words and Phrases

1. 栄養(学)　　2. …を証明する　　3. 無関係の
4. …のために　　5. …とたたかう
6. 不足　　7. おおよそ　　8. …を維持する
9. …を制限する　　10. 長い目で見れば

Questions

1. He tried to disprove some diet methods that claimed calorie-counting was irrelevant and unnecessary for the sake of weight loss (, and that watching what we eat was important).

解説 質問文は「マークは何を反証しようとしたか」である。第1段落5文目の those diet methods が指すものは，その前の文で説明されている。

2. He ate a serving of vegetables, a protein drink, and a multivitamin every day.

解説 質問文は「トゥインキーダイエットの間に，マークはジャンクフード以外に何を食べたか」である。第2段落2文目を参考に答えを作る。other than ...「…以外に」

3. The percentage [amount] of his body fat dropped from 33.4 to 24.9 percent.

解説 質問文は「マークの体脂肪率に何が起こったか」である。第3段落5文目が答えになる。

4. No, the writer doesn't. Because the writer thinks we should think more about whether junk food is really healthy in the long run.

解説 質問文は「筆者はトゥインキーダイエットが信頼できると思っているか」である。最終文で，筆者はジャンクフードが長期的に見て本当に健康的なのか懸念を投げかけている。

Express Yourself

例・和訳

Hamburgers: I recommend rice and miso soup because they are healthier than hamburgers. We chew more when we eat rice than when we eat bread, and soybeans are less fatty than meat. (31 words) （ハンバーガーよりも健康によいので，私はごはんとみそ汁をおすすめします。ご飯を食べるときのほうがパンよりもよく噛みますし，大豆は肉よりも脂肪分が少ないからです。）

Coke: I would recommend green tea instead of Coke. This is because green tea is said to kill some bacteria. It is useful for preventing diseases. (25 words) （私はコーラの代わりに緑茶をおすすめします。緑茶は殺菌作用があると言われているからです。それは病気を防ぐのにも有効です。）

Lesson 17

Words and Phrases

1. …に反して　　2. たくさんの…　　3. accident
4. 思い浮かぶ　　5. AからBを連想する
6. 負担　　7. 疲れている　　8. …を促進する
9. 安全(性)　　10. 今のところ

Questions

1. They are most likely to be popular in India.

解説 質問文は「グラフ2によれば，自動運転車が最も人気になりそうな国はどこか」である。「自動運転車を使いたいか」という質問に「はい」と答えた割合が最も高い国はインドである。

2. They would not feel stressed and exhausted.

解説 質問文は「クリスのレポートによると，自動運転車を利用することで貨物運転手はどのように感じないか」である。第1段落最終文に，truck drivers would not feel stressed and exhausted because ... とある。

3. Because many people in Japan are hesitant to use them.

解説 質問文は「和真のレポートによると，なぜ日本では自動運転車がすぐには普及しそうにないのか」である。第1段落3文目の so の前後の関係に注目する。

4. Because a human driver should always be ready to intervene and take control of the car when necessary.

解説 質問文は「なぜ日本では自動運転車を使うために人間の運転手が必要なのか」である。和真のレポートの第2段落3・4文目に注目する。

Express Yourself

例：In my opinion, self-driving cars will become usual in Japan if completely safe ones are developed. Some people are worried about who will take the responsibility for traffic accidents caused by self-driving cars. If we can avoid this situation, self-driving cars will become popular. (44 words)

別解：A self-driving car may not be affordable for most people because it will be extremely expensive. Also, at the moment the traffic infrastructure and laws are not designed for self-driving cars. Therefore, I believe self-driving cars are unlikely to become widespread in Japan soon. (44 words)

和訳 私の意見では，完全に安全なものが開発され
たら，自動運転車は日本で普及すると思います。
自動運転車が起こした交通事故の責任をだれがと
るのか不安な人がいます。このような状況を避け
ることができれば，自動運転車は人気になるでし
ょう。

別解：自動運転車は非常に高額になりそうなので，
ほとんどの人は購入できないかもしれません。ま
た，交通インフラや法律は現時点で自動運転車に
合わせて設計されていません。そのため，自動運
転車はすぐに日本で普及しそうにないと思います。

Lesson 18
Words and Phrases
1. 10年間　　2. 織物　　3. 不足している
4. 撤退する　　5. 契約　　6. …を捨てる
7. sew　　8. …に頼る　　9. …を始める
10. その間に

Questions
1. Maruo Clothing did.

解説 質問文は「岡山がデニムの聖地となるのにも
っとも貢献したのはどの企業か」である。第2段
落3文目に，... one single company, Maruo
Clothing, ... played an important role in
making Okayama a denim mecca. とある。

2. Because two big textile companies (, TORAY
and TEIJIN,) started selling a better
polyester called Tetoron.

解説 質問文は「なぜマルオは制服事業から去った
か」である。第3段落3・4文目を参考に答えを
作る。繊維大手が売り始めたテトロンという商品
に対して，質的な競争力を保てなかったのである。

3. They created an original line called BIG
JOHN (by using them).

解説 質問文は「マルオはB級のデニム生地を使っ
て何をしたか」である。第4段落3文目を参考に
答えを作る。

4. It was planned to celebrate Kojima's history
and brands and attract more tourists.

解説 質問文は「なぜ『児島ジーンズストリート』は
計画されたのか」である。第6段落1文目の in
order to ～ 以下を読み取る。

Express Yourself
例：Place: Kyoto

Kyoto was established as the capital of Japan
in 794. Since then, Kyoto has acted as a
center of politics, learning, and religion for a
long period of time. There are many
traditional temples and shrines. So far, 17 of
them have been registered as World Heritage
Sites. （48 words）

和訳 京都は794年に日本の都として制定されまし
た。それ以来，京都は長い間，政治，学問，宗教
の中心地として機能してきました。そこには伝統
的な寺や神社がたくさんあります。これまで，そ
のうち17件は世界遺産に登録されています。

Lesson 19
Words and Phrases
1. 明らかな　　2. …で構成される
3. 憂うつ，うつ病　　4. 不安　　5. 感情[情緒]の
6. military　　7. …を利用する　　8. 要するに
9. …を刺激する　　10. 特徴，特性

Questions
1. Because it offers a variety of benefits.

解説 質問文は「なぜ音楽は治療法として使われる
のか」である。第2段落1文目を参考に答えを作
る。

2. It is used for improving the quality of life for
people with physical health problems.

解説 質問文は「精神と情緒の健康を促進すること
に加えて，何のために音楽療法は使われるか」で
ある。第2段落最終文を参考にして答えを作る。

3. It is the same as other organs in that it
becomes sharper and more highly developed
when it is exercised.

解説 質問文は「どのような点で脳は他の臓器と同
じなのか」である。第6段落2文目を参考に答え
を作る。ここでは，in that S＋V「SがVすると
いう点で」を使うとよい。

4. We should listen to songs with a slower
tempo and a more predictable structure.

解説 質問文は「一般的に，リラックスしたいとき
はどのような音楽を聞くべきか」である。第7段
落最終文を参考に答えを作る。

Express Yourself
例：I love *I Don't Want to Miss a Thing* by
Aerosmith, and I often listen to it when I feel
sad. I like the lyrics of the song and I feel
encouraged when I hear it. Ballad songs
really soothe my feelings. （42 words）

和訳 私はエアロスミスの『ミス・ア・シング』が大
好きで，悲しい気持ちのときによく聞きます。私
はその曲の歌詞が好きで，それを聞くと励まされ
ます。バラード曲は本当に私の気持ちをなだめて
くれます。

Lesson 20
Words and Phrases
1. 食べられる　　2. …の原因になる　　3. 飢餓

4. …と何の関係もない　　5. 控えめな
6. 余った　　7. 貧困　　8. 法的に
9. 欠くことのできない　　10. 持続的に

Questions

1. Because many people in the world are suffering from starvation.

解説 質問文は「なぜまだ食べることができる食べ物を捨てることが残念なのか」である。第1段落4文目のconsidering …に注目。it is a shame …と考える根拠が記述されている。

2. Because they falsely believe that best-before dates on package labels indicate food safety.

解説 質問文は「なぜアメリカ人は毎年何十億ポンドもの食べ物を捨てるのか」である。第2段落2文目のbecause以下に注目する。

3. It can help to solve the problems of food waste and poverty (at the same time).

解説 質問文は「『フードシェアリング』はどんな社会問題を解決することに役立つか」である。第4段落6文目を参考に答えを作る。This kind of serviceとは，前の文に "food sharing" の一例として示された，レストランなどで余った食品を必要な人に供給するサービスである。

4. A law requiring supermarkets to donate surplus foods to charities or use them as animal feed was.

解説 質問文は「フランスではどのような法律が定められたか」である。第4段落最終文のIn France, supermarkets are legally required to ～ に注目する。

Express Yourself

例：I want to develop an app that can help connect us with local supermarkets so that surplus food is not disposed of. This app will tell us which foods are about to expire so that we can buy them with the app at discount prices. (45 words)

和訳 私は，余った食品が処分されることがないように私たちと地元のスーパーマーケットをつなぐ助けになるアプリを開発したいと思います。このアプリはどの食品が賞味期限が切れそうか私たちに教えてくれて，私たちはそれらをアプリで割引価格で買うことができます。